Overcom the Odds

Gail Devers

Bill Gutman

RSVP
RAINTREE
STECK-VAUGHN
PUBLISHERS
The Steck-Vaughn Company

Austin, Texas

Published by Raintree Steck-Vaughn Publishers,
an imprint of Steck-Vaughn Company

Developed for Steck-Vaughn Company by
Visual Education Corporation, Princeton, New Jersey
Project Director: Paula McGuire
Editor: Marilyn Miller
Photo Research: Marty Levick
Electronic Preparation: Cynthia C. Feldner
Production Supervisor: Barbara A. Kopel
Electronic Production: Lisa Evans-Skopas, Christine Osborne
Interior Design: Maxson Crandall

Raintree Steck-Vaughn Publishers staff
Editor: Helene Resky
Project Manager: Joyce Spicer

Photo Credits: **Cover:** © Denis Paquin/AP/Wide World Photos, Inc.;
4: © Eric Risberg/AP/Wide World Photos, Inc.; 7: © Deither Endlicher/AP/Wide World Photos, Inc.;
8: © Denis Paquin/AP/Wide World Photos, Inc.; 10: © Michael Poche; 13: © ALLSPORT USA;
16: © Focus on Sports; 19: © Tim Rue/AP/Wide World Photos, Inc.; 20: © Tony Duffy/ALLSPORT USA;
26: © David Cantor/AP/Wide World Photos, Inc.; 30: © Tony Duffy/ALLSPORT USA;
31: © James Meehan/ALLSPORT USA; 33: © ALLSPORT USA;
35: © Jim Sullry/AP/Wide World Photos, Inc.; 38: © Gary M. Prior/ALLSPORT USA;
39: © Bob Martin/ALLSPORT USA; 40: © Thomas Kienzle/AP/Wide World Photos, Inc.;
41: © Richard Drew/AP/Wide World Photos, Inc.; 42: © Mike Powell/ALLSPORT USA

Library of Congress Cataloging-in-Publication Data
Gutman, Bill.
    Gail Devers / Bill Gutman.
        p.   cm. — (Overcoming the odds)
    Includes bibliographical references (p.   ) and index.
    Summary: The story of the courageous woman who overcame debilitating illness
to go on to become an Olympic gold medalist in track and field events.
    ISBN 0-8172-4122-1 (hardcover)
    ISBN 0-8172-8003-0 (softcover)
    1. Devers, Gail, 1966– —Juvenile literature.   2. Runners (Sports)—United
States—Biography—Juvenile literature.   [1. Devers, Gail, 1966–
2. Runners (Sports)   3. Women—Biography.   4. Afro-Americans—Biography.]
I. Title.   II. Series.
GV1061.15.D49G88   1996
796.42′092—dc20
[B]   95–49416
                                                                                                              CIP
                                                                                                               AC

Printed and bound in the United States
3 4 5 6 7 8 9 0   WZ   99 98

Table of contents

Chapter 1

Olympic Triumph

The runners stood nervously at the starting line. Each was lost in her own thoughts, already running the race in her mind. For all of them, it was the biggest race of their careers, the Olympic 100-meter-dash final.

For Gail Devers, the American standing in lane two, the race was even more important. Neither Gail, nor anyone else, thought she would even be there. Less than a year and a half earlier, doctors were close to amputating both her feet. Just being at the starting line of the Olympic 100-meter-dash final was a miracle in itself.

The Olympic Games are the most important competition in track and field. Athletes from all over the world work hard for four long years hoping to triumph at the Olympics. The year 1992 marked the twenty-fifth (XXV) Olympiad. It was being held in Barcelona, Spain. Athletes from 172 nations were competing. Only the very best would make it to the

Gail shows off her gold medal after winning the women's 100-meter race at the 1992 Olympics.

finals in each event. Now eight women stood ready to run in the 100-meter-dash final. Each had her own reason for wanting to win.

The 100-meter dash is a fast race. Runners who race such a short distance at full speed are called sprinters. If the world's best women sprinters are in the 100-meter dash, the winner will usually break the tape in under 11 seconds. It is a race that requires a huge amount of energy released in an almost explosive fashion. The best sprinters must combine strength, speed, and concentration in order to win.

Top competitors are closely matched. It is important to get off to a very fast start, maintain top speed, then be ready to give a final, exhausting burst in the last few yards. There are no second chances.

Sprinters must be very powerful athletes. The men are usually heavily muscled in the legs, arms, and shoulders. Some look more like football players than like the fastest runners in the world. The women must have powerful thighs and calves and also be very strong in the arms and shoulders.

Most experts saw the 1992 women's 100-meter final as a toss-up. They expected the winner to be one of four runners—Gwen Torrence of the United States, Irina Privalova of Russia, Juliet Cuthbert of Jamaica, or Merlene Ottey of Jamaica.

Finally, the runners knelt down at the line, got set . . . and the gun sounded! The race was on.

Chapter 2

A "Leave It to Beaver" Family

No one can predict from the beginning who will become an Olympic champion. Some competitors come from athletic families. But that doesn't mean they will be great athletes. To be a great athlete, a person first has to have natural ability. But he or she must also have a very strong desire to develop the ability. And then the person must have the will to keep going when things look the worst.

Yolanda Gail Devers was born in Seattle, Washington, on November 19, 1966. Gail's father, the Reverend Larry Devers, was a Baptist minister. Her mother, Alabe, was a teacher's aide at an elementary school.

When Gail was still young, the family moved to San Diego, California. That's where she grew up. The Devers were a family of four. Gail had one brother with the unusual name of Parenthesis. He was 14 months older than she. The family was always very close and did many things together.

"We were a 'Leave It to Beaver' family," Gail has said, referring to the name of a television comedy series from the 1960s that portrayed a "typical"

American family. "We had picnics, rode bikes, and played touch football together. My father and brother played the guitar together."

Gail was a typical "good kid."

"I never tested my parents; my brother sometimes did," she said. "I used to call him a rebel without a cause. When it started to get dark, we had to be in the house before the streetlight stopped flickering. My brother hated that rule. I'd be a little mother, tugging him, explaining to him that later he'd understand."

Alabe Devers teased her daughter about her mothering ways. But Gail took life seriously even back then, and it has carried over to her track career.

Gail was a good student and always loved to read. When she was just ten, Gail was already helping some of her friends with their reading during the summer. Gail liked teaching so much that by the time she started high school, she decided to be an elementary school teacher when she grew up.

At that point, athletics were not really part of Gail's life. She played sports with her family but strictly for fun. Her happy childhood left her eager to learn and to help others.

Here's the California high school Gail attended. In her sophomore year at Sweetwater, she decided to take up running.

Chapter 3

A Star in the Making

In the fall of 1980, Gail Devers was a sophomore at Sweetwater High School in National City, California. She had never really run any track events at all. But that year she decided to take up running for the first time. She began doing some distance running, cross-country style. Slowly, however, Gail began to realize that she had real speed.

Unfortunately, Sweetwater High had no track coach. Students interested in the track team were left to work out on their own. It wasn't until her junior year that Gail began to make a mark in track. She still didn't know how good she could be. But Gail enjoyed running and competing against girls from other schools.

In some meets she would be the only competitor from Sweetwater. "It was the loneliest feeling in the world," Gail recalled. "I used to be really shy back then. My father used to have to stand on the field until I got ready to go out to the track, and then when I got back, he had to be right back there where I left him. It's just because I was there all by myself and didn't know anyone. No one ever spoke to me. But I understood. Everyone had their teams."

Even without a coach, Gail was becoming a fine sprinter. As a junior in 1983, she ran the 100-meter dash in a personal best of 11.69 seconds. This was a very good time for a high school sprinter. Gail was also beginning to try the 100-meter hurdles. That was a much more difficult event to master.

A hurdler must be a very fast runner—a sprinter. But she must also be able to jump ten hurdles, each of which is 33 inches (84 cm) high. So a hurdler must have good timing. She also must have the technique to go over the hurdles and land running at full speed.

As a senior in 1984, the 17-year-old Devers began making track news. Still working alone, she racked up some good times. While she remained much better in the 100-meter dash than in her other events, she was also improving as a hurdler and was a fine long jumper.

Gail was so good that she won the San Diego sectional team title for Sweetwater High all by herself! She was in a number of events and received enough points to beat any other team's total. That summer, Gail also won both the 100-meter dash and 100-meter hurdles at the California High School Track Championships. And she finished second in the long jump.

Gail then went to the National Junior Championships. Against the best high school girls in the country, she finished second in the 100-meter dash.

Then, at the Pan American juniors meet, Gail placed third in the 100-meter dash.

Her natural track talent and excellent academic record earned her a scholarship to the University of California at Los Angeles (UCLA). She went there in the fall of 1984.

When Gail entered UCLA, she had a personal best time of 11.51 seconds in the 100-meter dash. Her personal best time in the 100-meter hurdles was 14.32 seconds. This was not good enough to compete against the best women in the world in these events. Yet waiting for her at UCLA was someone who thought she could be a world-class athlete. He was the new women's track coach, Robert Kersee.

Bobby Kersee, the new women's track coach at UCLA, thought that Gail could be one of the world's best female runners.

At first Gail knew the coach only by name. At the United States Olympic trials in the summer of 1984, she asked sprinter Valerie Brisco to point out Robert Kersee. Gail was directed to a thin 30-year-old black man with an almost wild look in his eyes.

"He was easy to spot," she remembers, "because he was screaming at the top of his lungs at Jackie Joyner. I said, 'Uh-oh, maybe I can wait to meet him.'"

Jackie Joyner was already one of the great female track stars in the world. "Bobby" Kersee was her coach. He would later also become her husband.

As a coach, Kersee was driven to get the most out of his athletes. As soon as he learned that Gail Devers was in the stadium, he sought her out. And he gave her a clear message.

For openers, Kersee ordered Gail to watch the 1984 Los Angeles Olympics, which were to be held later in the summer very carefully. He also said that she had to begin to make a mental transition from high school champion to world-class athlete. He told her he could already see her breaking the U.S. record in the 100-meter hurdles and that she would make the 1988 Olympic team. And he said, flat out, that she would be ready for a gold medal in 1992.

Gail simply stared at Bobby Kersee. She still remembers what she felt just then.

"He had all these visions of years and years ahead," Gail said. "I could see he was crazy."

But Bobby Kersee wasn't crazy. He was about to change Gail Devers' life. Kersee knew a special athlete when he saw one. He believed that it was his job to get the best from each of them.

"It scares me," he once said, "the responsibility that comes with such athletes. I tell them, 'I'm not going to physically or mentally harm you. No scars. Hard work. Pain, sure. No scars.'"

Bobby Kersee began working with Gail. No one had ever worked like this with her before. Her times began coming down almost immediately. Gail had already watched Valerie Brisco win three gold medals at the 1984 Olympic Games. And Bobby Kersee had coached Brisco. So Gail began to really trust her new coach.

As a first-year student in 1985, Gail finally ran in her first NCAA Collegiate Track & Field Championships. She finished sixth in the 100-meter dash, the 200-meter dash, and the 100-meter hurdles. Her times in those events were 11.19 seconds, 23.12 seconds, and 13.16 seconds. She was getting close to world-class—that is, being able to run with the world's best female competitors in these events.

A year later, Gail was ranked seventh in the United States in both the 100-meter dash and the 100-meter hurdles. In the NCAA championships that year, she entered just the hurdles and the long jump. Gail placed fourth in the hurdles and second in the long jump.

By 1986, Gail was ranked seventh in the United States in the 100-meter hurdles for women.

Then, in 1987, she made a real breakthrough. That was the year Gail achieved a world ranking for the first time. Her 10.98 time in the 100-meter dash gave her a second-place finish in the NCAAs. Then, she won the 100-meter dash at the Olympic Festival and also at the Pan American Games. The result was a number-two ranking in the United States and number-seven ranking in the world in that event.

By this time, Bobby Kersee knew he had a real star in the making. "It may take a while for the bulb to go on in Gail's head," Kersee said, "but once it does, and she sees what she can do, she's unstoppable."

The coach meant that Gail had to begin by believing in herself. Any self-doubt in events decided by hundredths of a second can mean the difference between first and second, third and fourth. But Gail seemed to be on her way.

As a sociology major at UCLA, she had always maintained good grades. Gail was on schedule to graduate in the winter of 1989. But before that, there were some exciting happenings in track. First, there was her senior track season at UCLA. Then, that summer the 1988 Olympic Games were to be held in Seoul, Korea. Most people, including Bobby Kersee, felt that Gail had a chance to make the team in two events—the 100-meter dash and the 100-meter hurdles.

Chapter 4

A Terrible Setback

By 1988, Gail's track career seemed to be right on schedule. This was just the way Bobby Kersee had seen it three years earlier. Meanwhile, Gail continued to improve. On April 19, she set an American record in the 100-meter hurdles with a 12.71 clocking. Jackie Joyner-Kersee broke the record on May 7, with a 12.70 finish. But Gail seized the record back two weeks later when she ran the race in 12.61 seconds at the Pacific Coast Conference Championships. There, she also won the 100 meters and the long jump.

Shortly afterward, Gail won the NCAA 100 meters. Although she finished a disappointing third in the hurdles, Gail was ranked sixth in the country in the dash and second in the hurdles. Next, she capped off her season by finishing second in the 100-meter hurdles at the Olympic Trials. Gail made the Olympic team in that event and began preparing to go to Korea in September. She was very excited. Things couldn't have been better.

But once in Seoul with the rest of the Olympic team, Gail began to feel ill. At first, she couldn't

Gail (right) beats out Yvette Bates of the University of Southern California to win the women's 100-meter hurdles at the 1988 Pacific Coast Conference Championships.

pinpoint the problem. It was just an overall feeling of not being right. The first place it showed was in her performance. During practice, she seemed sluggish. She didn't have any bounce in her legs. In the quarterfinals of the 100-meter hurdles, she finished a disappointing fourth. If Gail didn't do better in the semifinals, she might not even have a chance for a medal.

But instead of doing better in the semis, she did worse. This time Gail finished eighth and last. Her time of 13.51 seconds was her slowest since high school. She was out of the finals. No one could really explain it. Maybe the pressure had been too much. Maybe she just wasn't ready for this kind of competition.

"Bobby [Kersee] was blaming himself for my bad races," Gail said. "He was racking his brain to figure out the mistake he had made in my preparation."

It was hard for Gail to watch stars like Florence Griffith-Joyner and Jackie Joyner-Kersee win a pair of gold medals apiece. But if Gail had regained her form right after the Olympics, then maybe people could have blamed her failure on the pressure. However, she continued to get worse. The bad races had nothing to do with Bobby Kersee's coaching, Gail's willingness to work, or the pressure of the Olympics.

Now one symptom of illness was appearing after another. Gail experienced migraine headaches, loss

Gail leaps over a hurdle at the 1988 Olympic Trials. She did well during the trials, but by the time of the Olympics, she was showing the first signs of illness.

of sleep, fainting spells, muscle injuries, loss of vision in her left eye, and uncontrollable shaking. None of the doctors could figure out what was wrong. In spite of this, Gail returned to UCLA and graduated in 1989 with a degree in sociology. But by then she was so sick that she could no longer compete in track.

Before the 1988 Olympics, 5-foot, 3-inch Devers weighed 115 pounds. That was her best weight for competition. Once she became ill, her weight fluctuated wildly. At one point she was down to 99 pounds. Then she put the weight on again. Gail's weight topped out at more than 130 pounds.

For nearly two years, the doctors played guessing games. At first, they thought she might be suffering from exhaustion. But rest didn't make her any better. Then, it was thought she might have diabetes, a disease in which the body cannot properly metabolize, or burn up, sugar. Diabetes can damage the entire body. But after many tests, the doctors also ruled out diabetes.

Meanwhile, Gail didn't compete in 1989 or 1990. She couldn't have, even if she had wanted to. The mysterious illness had made her too sick. It wasn't until late 1990 that her doctors finally realized what had been causing Gail's symptoms. She had Graves' disease, a form of hyperthyroidism. It is a rather rare illness.

Hyperthyroidism involves the thyroid gland. The gland is located toward the side of the neck and secretes a hormone that regulates growth. Graves' disease is caused by excessive secretion of the growth hormone from the gland. Gail had many of the symptoms of this illness. But the symptoms aren't the same for everyone. That's why the disease was so hard for the doctors to diagnose.

But diagnosing the disease was only part of the problem. Now Gail and her doctors had to decide how to treat it. Graves' disease can usually be controlled with medication. The first medication doctors wanted to try was a beta-blocker, but it was on the Olympic banned list. Athletes taking this kind of drug couldn't compete. So Gail refused to take the drug. Instead, she decided to try radiation, another method of treatment.

The radiation treatment was a disaster. It helped control the disease, but the side effects were awful. The radiation began eating away at other tissue in Gail's body, especially her feet.

"My feet were swollen and oozing yellow fluid," she said. "I had little holes all over my skin."

Gail's parents had to move in with her because she could do little for herself. They even had to carry her into the bathroom because her feet couldn't bear her weight. The pain was almost unbearable. Several doctors felt the only way to help her would be to amputate both her feet. Some thought it should be done almost immediately, within 48 hours.

At this point, neither Gail, nor her family, nor her many friends were thinking about her track career. What was more important now was simply to save Gail's life and return her to good health. Fortunately, one of her doctors finally realized that it was the radiation that was causing her foot problems. He ordered it stopped immediately.

After Gail was put on another medication, her overall health improved. Her feet also began to heal, very slowly. In spite of the change for the better, almost no one considered Gail Devers a competitive force on the track any longer. It was too bad, some said. Had Gail stayed healthy, she might have had a good chance for a gold medal at the 1992 Olympics. But one person had not given up hope.

Chapter 5

Coming Back

Within a month after the radiation treatment ended, Gail was able to walk again. That was enough for Bobby Kersee. He insisted she come out to UCLA and "work out." At first, Gail thought he was kidding. She couldn't even put a pair of sneakers on her sore feet. But Kersee didn't think it was too early. So in late March, Gail came out to the UCLA track.

Her "workout" was a slow walk around the quarter-mile track. And Gail had to do it wearing just socks. Yet she did it. For Bobby Kersee, that was step one.

At Kersee's urging, Gail continued to come out to UCLA every day. Pretty soon she was able to put on a pair of track shoes. Then, she was jogging lightly. Next, she was striding. In a couple of weeks she began to sprint. Gail's amazing progress was like a miracle.

But the question remained whether she could regain anything close to her former speed and skill. Bobby Kersee thought she could. By May, he insisted Gail begin jumping easily over the hurdles. The new medication had stabilized her system. And her feet had healed almost completely. Gail soon found she could take the hurdles again. In addition, much of her old speed seemed to be back. Kersee wasted no time. On May 11, in Modesto, California, Gail ran her first 100-meter-hurdles event since her recovery.

Gail didn't win the race, but she took the hurdles cleanly. Both her form and speed were good. Gail finished in 13.28 seconds. She had run a slightly faster time in her first year at UCLA in 1985. But that wasn't the important thing. Gail had proved she could still run the hurdles. She had also done this in close to world-class time. Her performance was being written up everywhere as a miracle comeback. Now Gail, too, believed her track career wasn't over. After that race, she began to work harder than ever to get back to her old form.

Kersee mapped out a game plan. Gail usually followed it closely. Sometimes, though, she questioned what her coach was doing.

"I'm one of those questioning people," she said. "I always ask why."

Kersee said he didn't always enjoy that. "I don't like to be questioned," he said, "but I welcome a serious request for the reason behind a given workout or technique. I stay a step ahead or they become the teacher, and I can't have that."

"He knows us all," Gail admitted, speaking about herself and the other women athletes Bobby Kersee coached. "He knows how far he can take each of us."

Coach Kersee wanted to take Gail all the way. He saw a return to his original vision, which had her ready to win the Olympic gold medal in 1992. And soon he had his star hurdler back on schedule.

Five weeks after running her 13.28 at Modesto, Gail was at the starting line for the USA/Mobil Championships. Most experts felt she hadn't been back long enough to win. But Gail had a good start and began taking the hurdles smoothly and with excellent form. In between hurdles her sprinter's speed was in evidence. She eased into the lead and seemed to grow stronger as the race wore on. When Gail crossed the

In 1992, Gail came to New York City to talk about the Mobil Indoor Championships. She also described her battle with Graves' disease. Gail said that she went through terrible times but now knew that she could conquer anything.

finish line in 12.83 seconds, she had won the championship. She still hadn't run as fast as she had in 1988 (a 12.61), but she was gaining on her record speed.

Now Gail pursued her track career with renewed vigor. She once again saw the chance to become the best, and she went after it. Gail focused on the hurdles for most of the summer. Her fastest 100-meter dash was 11.29 seconds. This was slower than she had run as a UCLA freshman in 1985. But she was still ranked ninth in the nation.

It was in the hurdles that Gail was making a name for herself again. In August, she traveled to the World Championships in Tokyo, Japan. This time, Gail finished second to Lyudmila Narozhilenko of the United Team (the former Soviet Union). Two weeks later, on September 10, in Berlin, Germany, she capped her comeback. Gail not only ran a personal best in the hurdles but also set a new American record. She won the race in 12.48 seconds. Gail ended the year ranked as the number-one hurdler in the United States and number two in the world.

Gail was now being praised for making the greatest comeback in track-and-field history. Considering that less than a year earlier some doctors had wanted to amputate her feet, no one would argue about that statement. The new medication controlled her Graves' disease. Still, Gail had to be very careful. She had to watch what she ate and also make sure she got plenty of rest.

That wasn't always easy for her. Gail had so much energy that she often had trouble sitting through a two-hour movie. Fortunately, she was able to relax when she read. Always an avid reader, Gail could speed-read and retain what she read. More important, reading kept her sitting and relaxing.

"I love long novels," she said. "I have to slow myself down. I'm always whipping through 500 pages in a day and a half. Then I'm mad when the book's over."

Reading wasn't Gail's only interest. "I love to crochet," she explained, "and I'm always doing crossword puzzles. I guess I'm just a grandmother at heart."

Gail also loved to collect stuffed animals, especially monkeys, and enjoyed studying about the human body. At this time, she also continued to talk about working with children someday. But it was typical of Gail that she didn't want to do it the usual way.

"I used to want to be an elementary school teacher," she said, "but now I think that by then it's almost too late to start. I really want to go after kids in the earliest years, when they're such sponges."

Gail's careful balance between resting and racing was working. Now she was poised to enter competitions in 1992, another Olympic year. The 1992 Olympic Games at Barcelona, Spain, would be a second chance for Gail to make her dreams come true.

Chapter 6

Going for the Gold

At the beginning of 1992, most observers felt that Gail would concentrate on the hurdles. She had not run too many sprints during her comeback year. Gail had often said that she ran the 100 meters just to polish her speed for the hurdles. But she began running more 100-meter races at the start of 1992, and her times were coming down.

"I'm starting to feel like a sprinter again," Gail said. Now there was talk of her trying for a double, medals in the 100-meter dash and the 100-meter hurdles. It was a large order to fill.

At the Olympic Trials, Gail was set to go in both events. Only the top three finishers in each event make the Olympic team, so you can't let down at all. Gwen Torrence was the favorite in the 100 meters, but Gail was considered America's number-one hurdler. Torrence won the 100-meter final trial in an impressive 10.97 seconds. Gail took second in 11.02 to make the team in that event.

Gail then went out and won the trials for the 100-meter hurdles in 12.55 seconds. This was her

Gail raises the flag after making the 1992 United States Olympic track-and-field team. Gail qualified for two events—the 100-meter dash and the 100-meter hurdles.

best time of the year. By this time, Gail was considered to be the number-one hurdler in the world. She was the favorite to take that event in Barcelona. As for the 100-meter dash, most experts felt she would be lucky to win a bronze medal (third place). Gail was just happy to be there after her ordeal with Graves' disease.

"My goal was simply to finish both races," she said.

The first final was the 100-meter dash. Few people expected Gail to win. But just before the race, her teammate and friend, Jackie Joyner-Kersee, came up to her and said, "You worked hard for this. You better get it."

That's what Gail did. She ran a great race. In the closest women's 100-meter Olympic final ever, she nipped four other runners to win the gold. Gail, Bobby Kersee, and Gail's family and friends were overjoyed at the victory. But there wasn't time for Gail to relax. She had to prepare for the finals in the hurdles. If Gail won, she'd be a double gold-medal winner. Only the greatest athletes can win medals in two different events.

At last, it was time for the finals in the hurdles. At the gun, a confident Gail burst out of the starting blocks. By the time she cleared the first hurdle, she was already in front. At 50 meters, it became clear that Gail was blowing the field away, increasing her lead. She looked like a sure winner.

By the time Gail approached the tenth and final hurdle, she was leading the race by several meters. That's a huge lead in a 100-meter race. But then what happened is every hurdler's nightmare. Gail's lead leg hit the tenth hurdle on the way up, causing her to stumble. She desperately tried to regain her balance,

Gail falls toward the finish line in the women's 100-meter hurdles during the 1992 Olympics. She has just stumbled on the last hurdle. Gail finished fifth.

stumbling forward and then kind of froghopping across the finish line. But she had lost her momentum. Four other runners beat her to the tape.

It was a devastating loss, especially since it came in the Olympics. But at least Gail had one gold medal. She took the hurdles misstep surprisingly well.

"My goal was simply to finish both races," she repeated. "I would have liked to have won a second gold medal, of course, but it just wasn't meant to be. Next time, though, I will finish the hurdles on my feet!"

The Olympics was Gail's only hurdle defeat of the year. But Bobby Kersee agonized over that loss. "Gail's stride length has to be shorter in the hurdles than in the 100 [meter dash]," Kersee explained. "Late in the 100 it's seven feet, but in the hurdles it can never be much more than six. We talked about that, but I didn't really concentrate on stride pattern as her key for the last three hurdles. Seeing her lead leg open up, seeing her go down . . . I do blame myself for not reminding her."

Gail could now safely say "next time." With her illness under control, she had beaten the best in the world in the 100-meters race. And in spite of losing in the hurdles, there were few who would dispute that she was the best hurdler in the world. In fact, by year's end, she was only ranked number three in the world in the 100-meter dash. But she was ranked number one in the world in the hurdles, despite her defeat in that Olympic event.

Gail returned from Spain with her gold medal and a plan for the future. Barring a flare-up of her illness, she would concentrate on track in 1993. She would try to become the best in the world in both the dash and the hurdles.

Gail was also already looking to the future outside of sports. "I would like to open my own day-care center someday," she said. "It will have to wait until I'm out of track, but I'm already studying child-care ventures."

Bobby Kersee has told her to "see" her day-care center. "That day-care center is real," he said. "It's out there, years from now, the way your gold in '92 was there in '84. . . . You have to see yourself opening that door, then work back through all the steps that got you there, and then see them."

It felt good to plan for life after her racing days. But Gail also knew she still had many more goals to reach as an athlete.

Chapter 7

World's Best

Although she had already won an Olympic gold medal, Gail began working hard for the 1993 season. Once again she had Bobby Kersee driving her.

Kersee felt that Gail was not quite aggressive enough. He explained, "Gail isn't exactly nonchalant, but she doesn't have the innate sprinter's nastiness. That's fine, dealing with her as a person, but not as a sprinter."

It may seem like an odd thing to say about a sprinter who had just won Olympic gold. But Kersee is a master psychologist who seems to know just how to get his athletes up for a meet. Gail decided to run indoors during the winter months. In 1992, an injury to a large muscle in her thigh kept her off the indoor circuit. Sprinters and hurdlers run shorter races indoors, usually 50 to 60 meters. This is because the size of indoor areas is too small for a 100-meter track. The shorter races suited Gail. She soon began winning indoors, too.

In 1993, Gail ran seven meets in February, losing only in Madrid, Spain. There, Irina Privalova beat

Gail in the 60-meter dash, setting a world record of 6.92 seconds. Gail was second, with an American record time of 7.05 seconds. She also set a personal best of 6.10 seconds in the 50-meter dash. Then Gail won the United States 60-meter championship, setting another indoor American record of 6.99 seconds. Next, she was going to have a return meeting with Privalova at the World Indoor Championships in Toronto, Canada. Once again, Coach Kersee went to work.

On February 27, 1993, Gail set an American indoor record of 6.99 seconds in the 60-meter dash.

"Before the 60 against Privalova, I think Gail was waiting for me to yell and carry on like I had in Barcelona," the coach said. "But I came at her from another direction."

This time, Kersee wrote Gail a letter. In it, he challenged her to take command of her emotions and focus on the race as she had at the Olympics. Before the Toronto race, Kersee looked at Gail as she warmed up and knew his strategy had worked.

"Watching her stretching after she read that, seeing how she carried herself, I said, 'It's there. It's over,'" Kersee said.

The coach was right. At the gun, Gail came blasting out of the starting blocks. She won easily, beating Privalova and setting a new American record by finishing in 6.95 seconds. Gail just missed the world record by .03 seconds. After the race, she referred to the note that Bobby Kersee had given her.

"Basically, Bobby told me that it's easy to win your first major championship, but tougher to win the following ones," Gail said. "He reminded me that it takes determination, willpower, and mental toughness. The World Indoor was something I wanted to do for myself. So it was a matter of me concentrating totally, really focusing on myself and getting the job done."

Gail seemed to be better than ever. When the outdoor season arrived, she said she would concentrate on the hurdles.

"This year my goal was to work on my speed in-doors, since the races were only 60 meters," she said. "Now, I'll work to transfer that speed over to the hurdles outdoors. I consider myself a sprinter at all times. Even when I'm in a hurdles race, I think of myself as a sprinter who happens to have to go over obstacles."

Bobby Kersee felt that Gail's natural speed was her biggest advantage as a hurdler.

"It's obvious there is no hurdler in the world as fast as Gail," he said. "The matter of control between hurdles, and how much time she spends in the air from takeoff to touchdown, will be the difference in how fast she runs the hurdles.

"But every hurdler in the world has got to be in-timidated by Gail because they all know rule number one: remove the hurdles and there's no way they can outsprint her."

Gail continued to run and win. In 1993, she competed in Europe during the summer. Her goal was to win at the World Championships in Stuttgart, Germany. Gail had to deal with a sore thigh muscle that caused her to miss a few meets. But by the time of the championships, she felt she was ready.

"By Stuttgart, I had no worries," she said. "I really didn't. I felt that the leg was healed. There's always aches and pains, and sometimes I feel we run better when we have something bothering us."

Once again, Gail would attempt a double, both the 100-meter dash and the 100-meter hurdles. Naturally, reporters reminded her what had happened during her hurdles race at the Olympics.

"It's like they say, 'If you fall off a bicycle, you've got to get back up and do it again,'" she said. "And this was my chance to get up and do it again. If it [a fall] were to happen again, I think that could scar you."

The 100-meter final came first. In that race, Gail and Merlene Ottey raced stride for stride to the finish line. They crossed at almost the same time. It was another photo finish. When Gail was awarded the victory, with a time of 10.82 seconds, the Jamaican officials protested the decision.

Gail (right) beats out Jamaica's Merlene Ottey to win the 100-meter dash in the 1993 World Championships.

Gail raises her arms to the crowd after her photo finish win over Ottey.

"I didn't know there was a protest until I was getting ready to go into the tent to get my clothes," Gail said. "But I have to deal with Gail. I figure I have enough to do to keep up with myself. I can't concern myself with things I have no control over. The only thing I had control over was running the race. I ran the race, the race was over. After that, it wasn't in my hands anymore."

Gail handled the controversy well. The decision held. She was the world champion. It didn't bother her that many fans applauded more for Ottey when they were awarded their medals. Gail still had the hurdles to run. She wasn't about to let anything upset her.

Gail admitted that she sometimes had problems transferring from the 100-meter dash to the hurdles. In the 100-meter dash, she let it all out. In the hurdles, she had to control her stride.

"In Stuttgart, I remembered Barcelona and played it wise," she explained. "In Barcelona, I was really trying to get back to being a hurdler right away and it didn't work. In Stuttgart, I didn't try to force the rhythm. I just tried to go slow. And in trying to go slow, my times ended up being faster because I wasn't trying to make myself hurdle at the 12.60 pace. I was letting it come."

By the time Gail reached the hurdles final, she was ready. She burst out of the blocks and took each hurdle cleanly. Her stride was just right. And as Bobby Kersee had said, no one could match Gail's speed. She

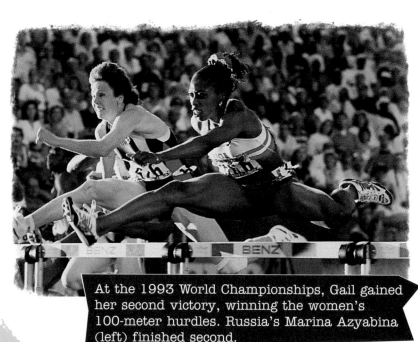

At the 1993 World Championships, Gail gained her second victory, winning the women's 100-meter hurdles. Russia's Marina Azyabina (left) finished second.

Great athletes like Gail win many awards. In January 1995, Gail received the SportsWoman of the Year Award from the U.S. Olympic Committee. Here she is before a news conference with Dwight Stones, three-time world-record holder in the high jump.

crossed the finish line first in 12.46 seconds, topping her own American record. She was now a two-time world champion.

It had been an incredible year. Gail lost just two races all year long. Her efforts were again rewarded when she was named the 1993 United States Women's Athlete of the Year. That had to be the crowning glory to her comeback, one of the greatest in all of sports.

"I think it was a good season," Gail said. "I accomplished the goals that I set out to accomplish. But while I did that, I'm never satisfied. I'm always looking for more, so I'm hoping the 1994 season will be even better."

Gail cut her schedule back somewhat in 1994. She had to deal with several muscle injuries, including a back-muscle pull, an injury that often affects sprinters and hurdlers. However, in 1995 Gail defended her 100-meter hurdles championship at the World Track and Field Championships held in Gothenburg, Sweden. Her long-term goal is to compete in and hopefully bring back more gold medals from the Olympics, being held in Atlanta in 1996.

Meanwhile, Gail continues to live a busy and active life. She has three pet rottweilers who are a big part of her life. Gail loves to talk about the dogs. She tells stories that make them seem like children. She continues to read a lot and passes time on the road doing huge jigsaw puzzles.

Gail is always writing her thoughts and plans down, some of which include her ideas for a day-care center. Her family and friends tease her about her note-taking. Her brother, a computer programmer, gave her a laptop computer to help with her notes. But she still prefers a pen and paper.

One of Gail's most challenging track goals is to beat the 12.21-second world record in the hurdles, set by Yordanka Donkova of Bulgaria in 1988. Another goal is to top the 10.49-second mark in the

Gail with two of her beloved dogs.

100-meter dash, set by Florence Griffith-Joyner, also in 1988. There is always something to aim for.

Gail still takes medication daily to control her thyroid gland. She also must be careful with her diet and rest. It's something she will never allow herself to forget, for many reasons.

"I definitely learned a lot from the illness," she has said. "I'm stronger as a person, and it's not hard for me to concentrate on the job at hand. I've said before that there's nothing that can come up in my life that I can't get over after going through what I did.

"My illness is something I never will forget. It taught me so much. I wouldn't wish it on anyone, but I'm happy I went through it. I think back to March of 1991, when I was wondering if I would ever walk again, let alone run.

"That's how I put it into perspective, and it just makes me very thankful to God. I must have a guardian angel watching out for me. Nothing bad can happen to me as long as I keep my faith in God and in myself."

Gail Devers' Personal
Best Times vs. World Records

Event	World Record	Set By	Gail's Best
60-meter dash	6.92 seconds	Irina Privalova, Russia February 11, 1993	6.95 seconds
100-meter dash	10.49 seconds	Florence Griffith-Joyner, U.S. July 16, 1988	10.82 seconds
100-meter hurdles	12.21 seconds	Yordanka Donkova, Bulgaria August 21, 1988	12.46 seconds

Gail Devers'
Greatest Victories

1. 1987 Pan American Games, 100-meter dash, 11.14 seconds, Indianapolis, Indiana

2. 1991 United States Championships, 100-meter hurdles, 12.83 seconds, New York City

3. 1992 United States Olympic Trials and United States Championships, 100-meter hurdles, 12.55 seconds, New Orleans, Louisiana

4. 1992 Olympic Games, 100-meter dash, 10.82 seconds, Barcelona, Spain

5. 1993 World Indoor Championships, 60-meter dash, 6.95 seconds, Toronto, Canada

6. 1993 United States Championships, 100-meter dash, 10.82 seconds, Eugene, Oregon

7. 1993 World Championships, 100-meter dash, 10.82 seconds, Stuttgart, Germany

8. 1993 World Championships, 100-meter hurdles, 12.46 seconds, Stuttgart, Germany

9. 1994 United States Championships, 100-meter dash, 11.12 seconds, Knoxville, Tennessee

10. 1995 World Championships, 100-meter hurdles, 12.68 seconds, Gothenburg, Sweden

Gail Devers'
Best Times and Rankings

Year	100-Meter Dash	U.S. Ranking	World Ranking
1983	11.69 seconds	not ranked	not ranked
1984	11.51 seconds	not ranked	not ranked
1985	11.19 seconds	not ranked	not ranked
1986	11.12 seconds	7	not ranked
1987	10.98 seconds	2	7
1988	10.97 seconds	6	not ranked
1989	did not compete, illness		
1990	did not compete, illness		
1991	11.29 seconds	9	not ranked
1992	10.82 seconds	2	3
1993	10.82 seconds	1	1
1994	11.12 seconds	5	10

Year	100-Meter Hurdles	U.S. Ranking	World Ranking
1983	did not run event		
1984	14.32 seconds	not ranked	not ranked
1985	13.16 seconds	not ranked	not ranked
1986	13.08 seconds	7	not ranked
1987	13.28 seconds	not ranked	not ranked
1988	12.61 seconds	2	not ranked
1989	did not compete, illness		
1990	did not compete, illness		
1991	12.48 seconds	1	2
1992	12.55 seconds	1	1
1993	12.46 seconds	1	1
1994	did not run event, injury		

Further Reading

Bailey, Donna. *Track and Field*. Texas: Raintree Steck-Vaughn, 1991.

Cohen, Neil. *Jackie Joyner-Kersee*. Boston: Little, Brown, 1992.

Gutman, Bill. *Track and Field*. North Vancouver, BC, Canada: Marshall Cavendish, 1990.

Parker, Steve. *Running a Race: How You Walk, Run, and Jump*. New York: Watts, 1991.

Rosenthal, Bert. *Track and Field*. Texas: Raintree Steck-Vaughn, 1994.

Index